THE NATURE OF THINGS

C000145211

THE NATURE OF THINGS

Poems from the New Zealand Landscape

Edited by James Brown ❖ Photographs by Craig Potton

CRAIG
POTTON
PUBLISHING

First published in 2005 by Craig Potton Publishing
98 Vickerman Street,
PO Box 555, Nelson, New Zealand
www.craigpotton.co.nz

Reprinted 2006, 2008

©Text: Individual poets

ISBN 978-1-877333-33-0

Scanning by Image Centre, Auckland, New Zealand
Printed in China by Midas Printing International Ltd

This book is copyright. Apart from any fair dealing for
the purposes of private study, research, criticism or review,
as permitted under the Copyright Act, no part may be
reproduced by any process without the permission of the
publishers.

CONTENTS

RUTH DALLAS

Deep in the Hills

Once I thought the land I had loved and known
Lay curled in my inmost self; musing alone
In the quiet room I unfolded the folded sea,
Unlocked the forest and the lonely tree,
Hill and mountain valley beach and stone,
All these, I said, are here and exist in me.

But now I know it is I who exist in the land;
My inmost self is blown like a grain of sand
Along the windy beach, and is only free
To wander among the mountains, enter the tree,
To turn again a sea-worn stone in the hand,
Because these things exist outside of me.

O far from the quiet room my spirit fills
The familiar valleys, is folded deep in the hills.

INTRODUCTION

On the whole I am suspicious of book introductions because they generalise, and I am suspicious of generalisations because they exclude or subsume detail. Yet generalisations are a necessity. Even from a particular standpoint in space and time the exterior world is always too multifaceted for us to experience in its entirety. So we sort: we exclude and subsume difference. We decide, when thinking about the New Zealand landscape, for example, that there are a number of generalisations that might usefully be made.

One is its variety. From the sub-tropical north to the fiords deep in the south, the country's terrain ranges from jagged lines of alps to undulating pastures, dense green interiors to thermal ventings, golden beaches to granite boulders. New Zealand is a long, narrow country; its three main islands extend north-south for 1600 kilometres and it is only 400 kilometres at maximum breadth. Its altitude ranges from coastal plains to 3754 metres at Aoraki/ Mt Cook, the highest point in the chain of mountains that runs up the South Island. Surrounded by the Tasman Sea and the Pacific and Southern oceans, and with Australia as the nearest landmass 1600 kilometres to the west, in New Zealand 'all roads lead to the sea' as poet Kapka Kassabova observed in her first book. Its climate is maritime, meaning windy and changeable — two adjectives that could also be applied to the land itself. A geologically young country, New Zealand is still being actively sculptured by floods, glaciers, volcanoes, plate tectonics, wind and sea. In 1991 the height of Aoraki/Mt Cook was reduced by 10 metres in a dramatic collapse.

Another general feature of the New Zealand landscape is its proximity to the population. New Zealand is not a large country. Even though the great majority of New Zealanders live in urban centres, unspoiled environments are rarely more than a couple of hour's drive away. And the urban centres themselves, especially those parts where most people live, the suburbs, often have a temporary feel to them. Street upon street of wooden houses sway with the wind and land, and seem constantly in battle with the natural world so that house maintenance is not merely about maintaining a structure, but also about maintaining a foothold on a fecund, dynamic landscape.

Related to population, a third feature of the New Zealand landscape is its relative emptiness. By European standards, New Zealand is sparsely populated. You don't have to go far to find solitude. But a low population density does have its downside. For a long time New Zealanders have been able to get away with some fairly casual attitudes toward the environment without overtly compromising the country's unspoiled image. The sorts of environmentally conscious practices that many countries with greater population densities have had in place for years are relatively recent arrivals on these shores. New Zealand's clean, green image may still be intact, but the reality is increasingly under threat.

Similarly, most New Zealanders are no longer the rugged individuals of the land exported by history. While many do enjoy the natural world, the experience is unlikely to involve straying too far from a car. But myth is a powerful thing. Decades spent converting all but the most infertile, inaccessible terrain into farmland have left an indelible imprint on the New Zealand psyche as well as the landscape. New Zealanders believe they are an outdoors nation, and to a large extent reality is what you choose to believe. So the landscape remains an important presence in many minds, even if its physical reality is, for many, little more than a hindrance to the daily commute. Perversely, if reality and image really are diverging, image may actually be gaining in precedence. Chris Carter, Minister for the Environment, commented in 2005 that 'New Zealanders are more and more seeing the landscape as part of who they are.' Clearly, images of New Zealand's pristine landscape endure in enough New Zealanders' minds for the tourist brochures not to seem increasingly remote and for the myth of the rugged, outdoors nation to be accepted currency throughout the world and, perhaps more crucially, in New Zealand.

Maori, as the original tangata whenua (people of the land), have connections with the land that go beyond even physical, emotional and historical attachments. For Maori, the landscape is alive with mythological and ancestral spirits, and as such at the very core of individual and tribal identity. Natural features play many different roles – from settings to principle performers – in the stories that make up Maori mythology. But not only is the landscape central to Maori culture and identity, as tangata whenua Maori are also inextricably part of what the land was, is and will be. The Maori concept of time sees the past as a constant presence within the landscape, the natural world thereby connecting both the spiritual to the physical and the past to the present and future. Hone Tuwhare's poem 'A talk with my cousin, alone' has the speaker engaging in casual conversation with the sun, sea and beachscape as well as his deceased cousin. The reference to 'Pakeha marine authorities' selling back 'ephemeral Maori land … lying somewhere between / low-water mark and high' eerily prefigures (the poem appeared in a collection in 1982) controversial government legislation passed in 2005, giving the Crown legal ownership of the seabed and foreshore – an act that many Maori see as little more than another land grab and a further erosion of their traditional rights as tangata whenua.[1]

So if the landscape is such a pervading presence in the collective New Zealand pysche, if not collective New Zealand life, it should come as no surprise to find it equally prominent in our art. Our poets in particular seem to have a deep-seated fascination with the landscape. I was once asked to look over an anthology of New Zealand poetry awaiting Russian translation and was struck by how strongly the landscape figured. But most of the poems were not actually about the landscape. Poems usually take place somewhere, and sometimes the landscape is merely a backdrop against which other subjects play out. Relationship poems, to take a common example, often take place in natural settings (frequently beaches), and while such settings may contribute greatly to the potency of the poem, they are clearly not the primary focus.

So what is a landscape poem? It would be extremely limiting if a landscape poem were only allowed to be a description of a landscape. In poems that are clearly about other things, the landscape can nevertheless sometimes be so present and pervasive that it becomes more than just an ingredient in the poem's mix. Andrew Johnston's 'The Sounds', for example, is certainly a relationship poem, but its evocation of the physical and aural environment of the Marlborough Sounds is so strong that to my mind it is also a superb landscape poem. Similarly, Kerry Popplewell's 'On Seeing the Red Hills Again' is about seizing life's opportunities while you have the chance, and yet because this is illustrated so splendidly through the protagonist's yearning for the Red Hills it too is a landscape poem of the highest order. Jenny Bornholdt's 'Make Sure' barely mentions a landscape at all, yet still manages to create one in the reader's mind.

Another issue that came up when trying to decide what constituted a landscape poem was how to treat poems about the weather. Rain, storms, clouds and sunsets are popular poetic subjects in their own right. Does New Zealand's changeable and often extreme climate constitute part of our landscape? After all the English translation of Aotearoa is 'land of the long white cloud'. And what about poems looking out to sea or gazing at the southern night sky? I decided that, with regard to the weather, the landscape is the landscape, so the climatic conditions had to interact with the landscape in some way. Luckily Gregory O'Brien's 'Storm Warning' mentions 'beacon and wind-turbine' allowing its southerly storm to be located in Wellington.[2] Similarly, I decided seascapes had to interact with the land. The southern night sky did, however, seem to qualify for exemption by virtue of being uniquely linked to the observer's land-based

1 The 'tangi-hanga' the speaker suggests may one day be banned is a traditional Maori funeral.

2 The poem also has a whole other level as a protest against the sale, by Victoria University of Wellington, of the painting *Storm Warning*, originally gifted to the university by artist Colin McCahon (for more on this see *Sport* 23).

position. New Zealand's night sky is New Zealand's alone.

A surprising number of poems are actually parts of longer sequences. Perhaps the most famous of these are Denis Glover's startling *Sings Harry* sequence, from which steps 'Lake, Mountain, Tree', and Allen Curnow's *Trees, Effigies, Moving Objects: a sequence*, which provides both 'A Dead Lamb' and 'There is a Pleasure in the Pathless Woods'. All the transplanted poems flourish independently of their original contexts, though readers are strongly encouraged to seek out those contexts in order to discover how the poems' colours change. Rhian Gallagher's 'Waitohi', for example, reveals different horizons when read as part of a sequence about pioneer aviator Richard Pearse.

Poems are made up of multifarious sounds and voices, and the poems accompanying the photos in this book are as varied in tone and texture as the New Zealand landscape itself. Yet interestingly, for all the sad, contemplative, humorous, cheeky and elated noises going on in the poems, it seems to me that behind many of them is a kind of silence. This is not the silence of the landscape – landscapes are, to differing degrees, usually full of sound – but a silence emanating from within the voice of each poem. It is the silence of awe, the silence of the ineffable, the silence of the unsayable. When confronted by something that has particularly caught our attention we sometimes say that it 'takes our breath away' or that 'words fail us'. Both expressions are intended to convey the extent of our amazement, and yet there is also something frightening within them, a hint of death and the breakdown of language or our ability to use it. Is this what the poems' noises are trying both to mask and express – a speechlessness that is beyond feeling, beyond consciousness, beyond words?

It is perhaps Craig Potton's photographs that are able to communicate this feeling most directly, partly because, being photographs, they are able to operate outside the constraints and consciousness of language, but also partly because presenting the unutterable is one of Potton's central concerns. Although poems can be as much about silence and space as sound and solidity, it is not as easy to speak a silence as it is to see one, and it is not easy to put into words the kind of silence that many of Potton's photographs suggest, which is a silence associated with what has become known as the sublime.

The sublime can be thought of as a response to the majesty of a landscape, a feeling we get when, in the presence of something greater than ourselves, we become acutely aware of our insignificance and impermanence. As such, to be in the presence of a sublime vista is to feel humbled, vulnerable and even frightened, and yet at the same time inspired, fortified and uplifted. Perhaps this is because sublime landscapes are so manifestly outside the realms of human endeavour they do not make us feel insignificant in petty, human ways. Our gaze is more likely to be one of admiration and respect for we are thankful that the universe and our position within it have been brought into proper perspective.

Sublime landscapes are not necessarily beautiful. They can be harsh, featureless and even ugly. Their key quality — majesty — is often a result of repetitiveness, remoteness, vastness and emptiness. On the south coast of Wellington there is a seal colony near a place called Red Rocks. The road ends and becomes a four-wheel-drive track squeezed between surf-pounded shingle and high, crumbling cliffs where flax and scrub cling for dear life against wind and erosion. It isn't particularly scenic and although the cliffs are steep and high, they are not quite grand enough to be truly majestic. Beyond the seal colony, however, the road branches and heads up the crumpling slope, eventually turning inland where the steep coastline is breached by a valley and stream. The outlook is desolate and sweeping: rocks and shingle cascade down the 200 metres to the shore. The power of the landscape and the forces acting upon it are suddenly immensely palpable. The perspective has subtly altered from the merely impressive to the quietly sublime, a transformation someone has, at some point, understood and, on a boulder overlooking the view, been moved to mount the following plaque: 'Mightier than the thunders of many waters, mightier than the waves of the sea, the Lord on high is mighty! Psalm 93.4' — beneath which is added 'God is always greater than all of our troubles.'

Because what is mightier than man has traditionally been called god, says Alain de Botton in *The Art of Travel*, in the presence of sublime landscapes it is not unusual, even in our secular age, to feel we are not just viewing the work of powerful natural forces but also somehow the mark of a deity. The inscription on the plaque overlooking the coast beyond Red Rocks captures this element of the sublime perfectly, and one can also sense it in Craig Potton's photographs. Many have the compositional rightness of Andy Goldsworthy's land sculptures. But there is no preordained staging — one cannot direct the clouds, the land, the light, unless one is a god, and Potton does not play god with the landscape even if his images might sometimes suggest a divine order. He does not even use filters.

His photographs are the result of a lifelong engagement with the landscape and the works of others similarly inspired by it — an elusive combination of *Moment and Memory*, as the title of one of his books describes. And it is at the intersection between this long association and heightened moments in the now that the boundary between photographer and subject appears to fall away.

I am looking into a forest at chaos: tangled lianes and strangely shaped trunks with scalloped bark. Abruptly angled branches clash in a discordant mess. I am deeply attracted to such disorder, often overwhelmed by its entropic liveliness. Subtle green shades resonate in and out of tangled ebony lines. Then something begins to emerge — I would hardly call it order, it's more complex — and collapses back into disorder if I look too hard. But if I tease it out and hold my concentration largely around its centre, a definite form starts to define itself. Much later (in a less excitable moment, or even on the light box) I will examine the edges of the picture frame and check that there are no distractions — but all that is done later and for now I walk in the living green, waiting …

Moment and Memory

Potton's images are an unusual combination of the ordinary and extraordinary. One is drawn to the far-flung, imperishable scenes where, under the gentle aegis of the lens, earth and sky exchange elaborate favours. But look closely at the smudges of cloud, the undulations of land and water, the fluctuating green, and it's surprising how often they seem somehow familiar. Potton's photographs are not, like so many idyllic tourist brochures, beyond the bounds of actual experience. You too have witnessed clouds uncannily aligned with the landscape, colour of a similar hue, light transporting water — or had you forgotten?

Potton's photographs also perform acrobatics with that most contentious of terms, beauty, by finding it in places that its most ardent pursuers might easily overlook. A harsh and repetitive landscape reveals, through Potton's lens, the sublime's grand design. Sometimes the weather is plainly foul, the light brooding. Sometimes the focus is small — a rock, a rift, a ripple. Many images compose themselves around a central point, with the elements leading the eye to it being extremely subtle — the density of foliage, the play of light and shade, the angle of entry. If the devil is in the detail, as the saying goes, so too is the deity.

To focus on the image accompanying Denis Glover's poem 'Lake, Mountain, Tree' is to be amazed at how well the poem seems to speak to it. It is almost as if the poem were written with the photograph in mind, or the photograph taken with the poem in mind. Not all the images and poems are so strikingly conjoined, but there is always connection, some detail in the image translating some sounding in the poem. Notice how the image accompanying Bill Manhire's poem 'Magpie Crooning' seems to '[swim] / in silence at the bottom of a wave'.

And so the general leads us back to the specific. We search for the examples, the details that sustain the overview. But we also look for the exceptions, the anomalies that stand outside it. We see from our own viewpoint and try to locate and articulate our own responses, our own patterns, for it is through these that we are also able to locate ourselves, to discover where it is we are coming from. The poems and images in this book are not so much a window, through which one might only see, but a doorway, through which imaginative readers might pass into their own slanted and enchanted hinterland, and, in so doing, glance back and glimpse themselves.

James Brown

DENIS GLOVER

Lake, Mountain, Tree

Water brimmed against the shore
Oozing among the reeds,
And looking into the lake I saw
Myself and mountains and weeds.

From the crystal uttermost ridge
Dwarfed was the river's course;
Cloud-shouting, to the world's edge
I rode a whole island for my horse.

Forlorn at the last tree,
Grey shingle bruised our bones;
But there holding tenaciously
Were roots among stones.

Knowing less now, and alone,
These things make for me
A gauge to measure the unknown
– Lake, mountain, tree,
   Sings Harry.

Collecting Pipi

I wrestle
in the sea's mouth
            for a handful of pipi.

One balances
between my knuckles.

They leave
            suckingly
and clatter
                        at the bottom
            of the bucket.

Quietly
            the sea feels
                        with a tongue
round the holes
            in her still-hidden
            gums.

She mutters under her breath
            to the tide

who it seems

            is always out
when you need him.

BRIAN TURNER

Crossing the Canterbury Plains

The field shines with the light of cut corn
                and quite far off
     a solitary pine needles a solitary cloud
but I don't care
     for we seem to be safe here
where nothing vexes the sky
        that's clear to the mountains
and beyond.
            When the sun shines
even autumn's haughty out here
        where a leaf might be blown a hundred miles
     and end up somewhere much the same.
That's plains, they
     make you bound to live
within the bounds of where you are;
         no next valley to explore,
       no nearby hills to scale
         looking for a hint of promised land.
We may travel to the ends of the earth
     and back again
         and never know whether
    the beetle hunched between stalks
       feels sorrow, or if the distant clouds
quivering with white light
         drift forever.

Hope

It is to do with trees:
being   amongst trees.

It is to do with tree-ferns:
mamaku, ponga, wheki.
Shelter under here
is so easily
understood.

You can see that trees
know how it is
to be bound
into the earth
and how it is to rise defiantly
into the sky.

It is to do with death:
the great slip in the valley:
when there is nothing left
but to postpone all travel
and wait
in the low gut of the gully
for water, wind and seeds.

It is to do with waiting.
Shall we wait with trees,
shall we wait with,
for, and under trees
since of all creatures
they know the most
about waiting, and waiting
and slowly strengthening,
is the great thing
in grief, we can do?

It is always bleak
at the beginning
but trees are calm
about nothing
which they believe
will give rise to something
flickering and swaying
as they are: so lucid
is their knowledge of green.

JAMES K. BAXTER

At the Franz Josef Glacier

The hot rust-coloured springs in the riverbed
Were dry, but a smell of sulphur

Haunted the trees along the faultline
Under the glacier face where the guide

Split with his ice axe a boulder of cunninghamite
And showed us the small rock garnets

Like blood drops. Brunner wrote of this country:
'March is a bad month to ford the rivers

On account of the moss that grows…' Yes, explorer,
Deerstalker, have to pass the needle's eye

To get where they are going. The griefs I carry
Are nothing. All men die. What sign

Can I leave on cairn or tree to tell
The next comer that my thoughts were human?

As red moss grows on the glacial stone,
Then thicker spores whose acid crumbles it

A little – then the seeds the birds may drop,
Making their own earth, sending down roots,

Cracking and rending the rock – so may my words
Give shade in a land that lacks a human heart.

JANET FRAME

The End

At the end
I have to move my sight up or down.
The path stops here.
Up is heaven, down is ocean
or, more simply, sky and sea rivalling
in welcome, crying Fly (or Drown) in me.
I have always found it hard to resist an invitation
especially when I have come to a dead end
a
dead
end.

The trees that grow along cliff-faces,
having suffered much from weather, put out thorns
taste of salt
ignore leaf-perm and polish:
hags under matted white hair
parcels of salt with the string tangled;
underneath
thumping the earth with their rebellious root-foot
trying to knock up
peace
out of her deep sleep.

I suppose, here, at the end, if I put out a path upon the air
I could walk on it, continue my life;
a plastic carpet, tight-rope style
but I've nothing beyond the end to hitch it to,
I can't see into the mist across the ocean;
I shall have to change to a bird or a fish.

I can't camp here at the end.
I wouldn't survive
unless returning to a mythical time
I became a tree
toothless with my eyes full of salt spray;
rooted, protesting on the edge of this cliff
— Let me stay!

VINCENT O'SULLIVAN

Still Shines When You Think Of It

Stood on the top of a spur once
the grunt before Sheila sharp beside him
a river shining like wire ten miles off
the sky clean as a dentist's mouth
jesus *Was* it lovely!
            and the hills folded and folded
again and the white sky in the west
still part of the earth
            there's not many days like that eh
when your own hand feels a kind of godsweat
fresh on things like they're just uncovered.

And not fifty feet from the spur
a hawk lifted
            and for two turns turned like one wing
was tacked to the air
            and then she's away
beak a glint as she's turning
so the grunt sighs like in church
and even Butcher
                  yes Butcher too
thinks *hawkarc curries the eye all right*
gives your blood that push
while the mind corrupts as usual
with 'proportion' 'accuracy' etcetera
those stones we lift with our tongues trying to say
            ah! feathered guts!
And she's closing sweet on something,
death, that perfect hinge.

It still shines when you think of it,
                  like that river.

26

Haiku (1)

Stop
your snivelling
creek-bed:

come rain hail
and flood-water

laugh again

MAURICE DUGGAN

In the Territory

Expecting this turning, this ascent
to open a clear vista to the coast
he confronts another range, more bush
across a valley of unpromising aspect:
the map is vague beyond this point.
The immediate problem is less the going
than the blisters and the pack-rash,
the usual trouble with constipation
and the absence of any clear horizon.

The momentum of his eager departure
pushes him forward through the lichened trees.
There is no direction but forward:
from here on his ordinary skills
assume proportions of an absolute routine
whose goal is this night's fire this night's sleep.
The magnitude of any day is now reduced
to one mile of scree, two cups of brackish tea
and the certainty of knowing no way back.

Nothing so grand or challenging as Terra Incognita,
no legend reading Here be Dragons,
just this unfriendly skim of river water,
tape of steel light, impassable canyon there,
and the grey incessant veils of persisting rain.
The map dribbles possibilities eastwards.
From this morning's doused and comfortless fire
to tonight's tongues of flame and steam of socks —
measure and description enough of this explorer's day.

LAURIS EDMOND

Lake Idyll
for Frances

Mount Tauhara, substantial as it is,
rose in the afternoon and settled,
poised without effort in a blue breath
of air, lake water, the remote snows

of Ruapehu: all blue. Gravity itself
became a sheeny vapour that entered
and transmuted every rock and scree
till earth flowered into light.

'Will you stay,' she said '– leave tomorrow
morning?' And at once arrangements, work
the clotted bulk that leans against
the days entered that rapt atmospheric

alchemy and was dissolved. All night
the water lapped outside my window,
new worlds forming hour by subtle hour
in movements of its liquid particles.

CHRIS ORSMAN

Ornamental Gorse

It's ornamental where it's been
self-sown across the hogback,

obsequious and buttery,
cocking a snook at scars,

yellowing our quaint history
of occupation and reprise.

The spiny tangential crotch,
gullied and decorative,

I love from a distance,
a panorama over water

from lakeside to peninsula
where it's delicate in hollows,

or a topiary under heavens
cropped by the south wind.

I offer this crown of thorns
for the pity of my countrymen

unconvinced of the beauty
of their reluctant emblem: this

burnt, hacked, blitzed
exotic.

BRIAN TURNER

Place

Once in a while
you may come across a place
where everything
seems as close to perfection
as you will ever need.
And striving to be faultless
the air on its knees
holds the trees apart,
yet nothing is categorically
thus, or that, and before the dusk
mellows and fails
the light is like honey
on the stems of tussock grass,
and the shadows
are mauve birthmarks
on the hills.

Make Sure

Make sure you fall in love with a man who you know will survive in
the bush.
This way, when he is three nights overdue from his trip and the
search and rescue team is out looking for him and the helicopter
has been called back because the weather is closing in and they're
interviewing you on television in a close-up camera shot, asking
you what you think his chances are – hoping you will cry and
your lip will tremble – you can look them straight in the eye
and say you *know* he will be all right, he has had plenty of
experience and he knows what to do, he was carrying plenty of
food and warm clothing and he is strong.
Even if he is hurt, you know he will be all right.
He's a fighter, you'll say. He won't give in.
But the weather is closing in, you must be worried, they'll ask.
You keep your resolve. He will be all right, you say.
I know he will.

IAIN LONIE

A Summer at Purakanui

Something in us too is ground
down all the time that can never
be made up again: look at these coarse
grains separate in the hand
that were held together in the kinship
of rock that lasts for ages—

                            look at the blackened
sticks of kelp and the bleached
broom twigs and the dirtied
wing of the gull
half covered in grey sand
and fluttered by the wind—

listen to the wind whisper
listen to the sea—
you'll hear a kind of cosmic breathing
in and out
then in and out again.
It too could dry up
and there be nothing: hard
for us to understand
who find this all too easy

the grinding of rock to sand
our walking away and saying nothing.

KENDRICK SMITHYMAN

Waitomo

Guides ask for silence, and have
no difficulty in getting their parties
to go quiet. At a dollar a head, nations
file underground. All shapes of age bow
their heads, step carefully after.
Go deep, go down to silence.

Bridal Chamber, and Cathedral,
play of fancy which wants to discover
limestone making metaphors, shadow likenesses
and shadow play. Here is Dog, there is
Camel. We call this the Modern Art
gallery, but go down
further, one more, a couple more flights.
A boat at a landing stage idles,
another will carry us, silently
animated through the grotto
where cannibal worms hunt, breed, age,
consume their partners, are consumed.

How this would have pleased Coleridge,
riding a verbless river, the dome,
darkness, glowworm haven
generously imitating, freely outdoing, stars.

I have been here before, without words.
After their climax of love people lie thus,
as though drifting dark waters, caverned.
If you speak, all the lights will go out.
Say nothing. She reaches for his hand,
he presses her finger. The boat slides
curving back to its landing.

A guide at the stage sweeps his lamp
over a pool. What is he looking for?

ALLEN CURNOW

A Dead Lamb

Never turn your back on the sea.
The mumble of the fall of time is continuous.

A billion billion broken waves deliver
a coloured glass globe at your feet, intact.

You say it is a Japanese fisherman's float.
It is a Japanese fisherman's float.

A king tide, a five o'clock low, is perfect
for picking mussels, picking at your ankle-bones.

The wind snaps at the yellow-scummed sea-froth,
so that an evanescence of irised bubbles occurs.

Simply, silverly the waves walk towards you.
A ship has changed position on the horizon.

The dog lifts a leg against a grass-clump
on a dune, for the count of three, wetting the sand.

There is standing room and much to be thankful for
in the present. Look, a dead lamb on the beach.

Waitohi

The hills give and lean in opposition,
the echo of contact – green
and the paper lightness of summer.
The wind tasking, the wavy footsteps
of heat crossing paddocks. Velocities.
The grass on bended knee,
the electricities of a cabbage tree.

Up in the air, and gullies, troughs,
hill-line drafts. The twilight
sweeping from wing-tip to wing-tip.

URSULA BETHELL

Candour

Everything was white this morning.
  White mists wandered all about the river-bed,
Grey clouds, light-infused, conveyed the morning,
  Covering with whiteness the wide sky overhead.

White, past belief, the high and snowy mountains,
  Phantom-like, visionary; whiteness upon whiteness
Of frozen foam from far celestial fountains
  Suffused with soft and universal brightness.

Everything was white, this morning,
  Untroubled, luminous and tranquil pure;
Bright as an affianced bride, adorning
Herself with white upon the plighted morning;
  Past all debate, all hazard, still, and sure.

RUTH DALLAS

In Central Otago

Seek foliage and find
Among cracked boulders
Scab of lichen, thyme.

Seek a burgeoning tree
Discover
Upended witches' brooms.

Seek grass and tread
Stiff sheet of ice drawn
Over the land dead.

Moon country.
No one could live here,
In the houses squat on shingle.

Fields scorched,
Snow gripping the mountains;
Nothing could recover

From such desolation,
Jack Frost's sheep-run,
Mirror of the bleak mind.

But come back in a month –
See blanketing the slits
And sockets of the land's skeleton

Square eiderdowns of peach-bloom,
Old crone, Plum, unpick
A feather mattress from a bald stone.

IAN WEDDE

To Ernst Dieffenbach

Once thrown up by the mysterious fires of the deep
They were soon again hid from our view, basalts,
Greenstones, trachyte, augitic rock, oxydated
Iron-clay, its summit a never-failing
Object of attraction when the morning or evening sun

Gilded its snowy summit with a rosy hue.
Cliffs of yellow clay embedded with the remains
Of trees still existing in the island, and a countless
Number of small streams, all the pebbles
Hard blue trap-rock. Here and there

Might be seen a majestic rimu pine, or rata,
Bearing crimson flowers. The country now
Began to rise a little, we scarcely ever
Obtained a view of the sun, at sunset a thick
Forest surrounded this place. Rats

Ran over us all night. Another
Bird is very common, and always screams –
Huei, huei, tierawak, tierawak. For the first
Time, covered with snow, but its summit hid
In the clouds. Vegetation had long ceased,

A supernatural spirit breathes on him
In the evening breeze, which gives birth to the poetry
Of infant nations – the old tales of the Germans.
How little benefit has resulted to barbarous tribes
Gradually, as if acted upon by a slow poison.

The Scene

Mountains nuzzle mountains
White-bearded rock-fronted
In perpetual drizzle.

Rivers swell and twist
Like a torturer's fist
Where the maidenhair
Falls of the waterfall
Sail through the air.

The mountains send below
Their cold tribute of snow
And the birch makes brown
The rivulets running down.

Rock, air and water meet
Where crags debate
The dividing cloud.

In the dominion of the thorn
The delicate cloud is born,
And golden nuggets bloom
In the womb of the storm.

So you don't belong, pohoot

What can you do about it, eh tree.
Suck the water and see, maybe—
send your roots out through rock,
tie yourself in knots to the bones,
spread a blanket for summer picnics.
Act confident, act like you're blossoming
like you have a lot to offer. Look as good
as you can—grey green in the lonely cold,
scarlet and proud in the heat. Open up,
take each day for what it's got. Take
a leaf, unfurl it, take the next, unfurl it.
What do pieces of paper have to do
with you, a tree, alone on the shore
already burning?

The Cave

In a hollow of the fields, where one would least expect it,
Stark and suddenly this limestone buttress:
A tree whose roots are bound about the stones,
Broad-leaved, hides well that crevice at the base
That leads, one guesses, to the sunless kingdom
Where souls endure the ache of Proserpine.

Entering where no man it seemed
Had come before, I found a rivulet
Beyond the rock door running in the dark.
Where it sprang from in the heart of the hill
No one could tell: alone
It ran like Time there in the dank silence.

I spoke once and my voice resounded
Among the many pillars. Further in
Were bones of sheep that strayed and died
In nether darkness, brown and water-worn.
The smell of earth was like a secret language
That dead men speak and we have long forgotten.

The whole weight of the hill hung over me.
Gladly I would have stayed there and been hidden
From every beast that moves beneath the sun,
From age's enmity and love's contagion:
But turned and climbed back to the barrier,
Pressed through and came to dazzling daylight out.

BRIAN TURNER

Far North

We came in a campervan
branded with the name Maui,
over a dusty, corrugated road
along the spines of scrubby hills
to the lighthouse above the Cape
known as Reinga. And gazing
across the burnished waters
of Spirits Bay
towards North Cape,
I felt the press of what's
behind me – the incredulous and the
comfortable; love and pain;
care and gratitude; generosity
and austerity; an urge for revenge;
the need to forgive:
all the battered baggage
of character, culture, denoting
a certain southern spirit.

Here the gulf between us
seems vast, the Tasman and the Pacific
buckling and slavering, whipped
by a blustery westerly.
The signposts below the light
point to places once exotic,
instructive – London, Sydney, etcetera –
places where we could be delivered
unto true culture and sophistication.
All's veneer now; it's here
or nothing, and there's a sense
that feelings count for more
than words, and that neither is merely
mere.

Spirits Bay. The name conjures, the bay's
a vision, the reality's in unreality.
And yet our spirits seem antic here
insisting that we take them with us
wherever we go, and the essence
of friends or confidantes, they
who mock and amuse us, embellishing
what's mutual and what's not.

We have our photo taken, my friend and I,
in front of the lighthouse,
the Cape below
arrowing north. We find it easy
to smile. I can see he's happy:
and for once
he isn't saying: 'My goodness,
you're smiling…'

MICHAEL JACKSON

Matukituki

It took time to get used
to how immense the mountains were

Some nights we could not sleep
for the sound of avalanches
above the cirque,
the grinding teeth
of the glacier

On New Year's Day
we walked to the river at first light —
two paradise ducks
flew away upstream
curuck caraark

Forded it hand in hand
the cold water flowing on
through us for hours afterward
our bodies made as one
with water and stone

I remember
the bewildering distances
that afternoon
how small you were
walking ahead with Isabelle and Bryn
while I hung back
to take notes:

Pines hoorrahharrr
a solitary bird
in a lost language like Aztec
tir ror ah ti ka

Now that you have gone
into that valley forever
I cling to names
like trefoil and sedge
sweet vernal, senecio

Crossing the river alone
to nowhere you are.

JOHN DICKSON

Small Apocalypse

I got up
in time
to see first light

and though I thought that light
would rise
with the rising of the sun

it rose, instead
from some ancient mineral darkness
that is

it rose from the earth
it rose through the clay & humus & the pale blind
    roots of the grass & trees
it rose, but I hadn't

the time, I swerved in-
side, ate breakfast, fed the cats;
and when the radio

came on, I heard a man claim
that a Kampuchean refugee was just
like his daughter, but

for this also, I hadn't the time
there was a bus to catch, there was work
and somewhere else

the sun, lost, was orbiting in silent turbulence.
Good morning,
I said

ALLEN CURNOW

There is a Pleasure in the Pathless Woods

When the green grenade explodes, does the kauri
experience an orgasm of the spent cone?
What is the king fern doing with its hairy knuckles?
Wildling and epiphyte, do they have problems too?
There's a reason for the spastic elbow of this taraire.
Look hard at nature. It is in the nature
of things to look, and look back, harder.
Botany is panic of another description.

ANDREW JOHNSTON

The Sounds

Rain, a restful place: a plain
negotiation led to this, one small
lit room, in lieu of a camera, and the
drowned valleys, windless, listening
to the rain, on leaf, on water
in winter. Disentangled thus, we touch

as if deciphering a prophecy, we touch
as ocean, held by the land, made plain
a difficult map, whose cove-smooth water
uncoils with travel, surrounds a small
arrival, a larger departure. Listening
to the sounds as we pronounce them, the

waves, the bright particulars, we hear the
way we've been so far, we touch
speech, our bodies fearless listening
devices. And days unravel as on a plain
a road will travel straight with small
perceptible corrections. But water

under the hand of the wind, and water
in darkness: things we see and cannot tell, the
sounds are full of these too, as small
fish, late, in a bell of light, touch
the surface once and disappear. It's plain
each morning, talking and not listening

how plain things aren't, how whether we're listening
or not, the sounds go on around us, and water
will erase all previous arrangements. It's plain
how prophecies succumb before the
evidence, words in sand that crumble at a touch,
that need to be unwritten or forgotten, and small

reliable ambitions fashioned, parts for a small
cast—two, who move from stage to stage, listening
to the places where their different futures touch.
Rain-fast, a stream falls, to clear salt water
where just such a lean crew rows, the
dinghy iffing and butting, a plain

afternoon. The small boat drums the mingling water;
the rowers, listening, will remember the
sounds, when they touch, that these days made plain.

KERRY POPPLEWELL

Seeing the Red Hills Again

Summer: and almost dusk
   and we, coming down
a rustbrown gravel road
to an estuary
where the Cascade river bends west
   to a guessed-at sea.

We paused by the saddle.
   Below, shining coil
upon coil of water
splayed over rough grass flats
under a pale sky glinting white
   between light cloud slats.

When we looked to the south
   seeking out both source
and course of the water's flow
from cold spring to salt wave
I saw them again; and I knew
   how few chances you have.

———————

Nothing disguised those hills —
   irresistible
irrefragable rock,
bare resonance of red,
their ultramafic slopes held no
   snow grass or herb bed.

———————

I met those contours first
   when, just seventeen,
a green and eager girl
bound up the swampy Pyke
glancing far north, ahead, I saw
   each raw, distant spike

glow dark, spent-flax-stalk pink —
   all right out of reach,
and each desirable;
then had to turn away
though intending, of course, to come
   on some later day

to climb upon that range.
   Now, strange as before,
and yes, more beautiful,
again they were *there* —
but only for others to cross.
   This loss I must wear

as emblem of all things
   once possible, now
not. How fugitive
those futures, stowed with care
in some high attic of the mind's
   cold, unkind, dry air.

CILLA McQUEEN

Low Tide, Aramoana

Sky with blurred pebbles
a ruffle on water

sky with long stripes
straight lines of ripples

sky-mirror full of
sand and long pools

I step into the sky
the clouds shiver and disappear.

thin waterskin over underfoot cockles here & there old timber
& iron orange & purple barnacled crab shells snails green
karengo small holes

I look up from walking at
a shy grey heron on
the point of flight.

oystercatchers whistle stilts & big gulls eye my quiet
stepping over shells & seaweed towards the biggest farthest
cockles out by the channel beacon at dead low tide

It's still going out.
I tell by the moving
of fine weeds in
underwater breeze.

takes a time to gather these rust & barnacle coloured whole
sweet mouthfuls

Low.
and
there's a sudden

wait

    ·

for the moment
of precise
solstice: the whole sea
                hills and sky
                wait

           ·

                and everything
                stops.

high gulls hang seaweed is arrested the water's skin
tightens we all stand still. even the wind evaporates
leaving a scent of salt

           ·

I snap out start back get moving before the new tide back
over cockle beds through clouds underfoot laying creamy
furrows over furrowed sand over flats arched above & below
with blue & yellow & green reflection & counter reflection

    ·

look back to
ripples
begun again.

GREGORY O'BRIEN

Storm Warning

If, cloud-laden, the weather teaches us
a windswept humility, our children teach us

a kind of responsibility to all that is not yet formed.
Beyond beacon and wind-turbine, the half-formed storm dictates

its warning. And while our blindness teaches us how to tell
a bombed out bridge (because our children in their wisdom

cannot) from a moonlit ridge, our mathematics suggests
storms have their structures too, and how the southerly

is responsible for more than a dim day's light, ice-trails,
the early delivery of children. But it is the distant percussion

of the inner ear, our deafness that will teach us and go on
teaching us until there is no blueness on the face

of the earth, that a storm warning is only once,
then all we are left with, the storm.

JAMES K. BAXTER

Poem in the Matukituki Valley

Some few yards from the hut the standing beeches
Let fall their dead limbs, overgrown
With feathered moss and filigree of bracken.
The rotted wood splits clean and hard
Close-grained to the driven axe, with sound of water
Sibilant falling and high nested birds.

In winter blind with snow; but in full summer
The forest blanket sheds its cloudy pollen
And cloaks a range in undevouring fire.
Remote the land's heart. Though the wild scrub cattle
Acclimatized, may learn
Shreds of her purpose, or the taloned kea.

For those who come as I do, half-aware,
Wading the swollen
Matukituki waist-high in snow water,
And stumbling where the mountains throw their dice
Of boulders huge as houses, or the smoking
Cataract flings its arrows on our path—

For us the land is matrix and destroyer,
Resentful, darkly known
By sunset omens, low words heard in branches;
Or where the red deer lift their innocent heads
Snuffing the wind for danger,
And from our footfall's menace bound in terror.

Three emblems of the heart I carry folded
As charms against flood water, sliding shale:
Pale gentian, lily, and bush orchid.
The peaks too have names to suit their whiteness,
Stargazer and Moonraker,
A sailor's language and a mountaineer's.

And those who sleep in close bags fitfully
Besieged by wind in a snowline bivouac—
The carrion parrot with red underwing
Clangs on the roof by night, and daybreak brings
Raincloud on purple ranges, light reflected
Stainless from crumbling glacier, dazzling snow,

Do they not, clay in that unearthly furnace,
Endure the hermit's peace
And mindless ecstasy? Blue-lipped crevasse
And smooth rock chimney straddling—a communion
With what eludes our net—Leviathan
Stirring to ocean birth our inland waters?

Sky's purity; the altar cloth of snow
On deathly summits laid; or avalanche
That shakes the rough moraine with giant laughter;
Snowplume and whirlwind—what are these
But His flawed mirror who gave the mountain strength
And dwells in holy calm, undying freshness?

Therefore we turn, hiding our souls' dullness
From that too blinding glass: turn to the gentle
Dark of the human daydream, child and wife,
Patience of stone and soil, the lawful city
Where man may live, and no wild trespass
Of what's eternal shake his grave of time.

HONE TUWHARE

A talk with my cousin, alone

And afterwards, after the shedding of mucus, the droll
    speeches and the hongi for my cousin in the box,
    we were called to meal at the long tables.
    But I hadn't come for that.

I could hear the Tasman combers shredding themselves
    nearby, wishing then for a cawing beak of sound
    to help me reassemble myself. Taking my shoes off,
    I trudge a steep dune; sand, a cool silken lisp
    spilling through my toes.

Bottomed on a hill of sand, I wondered wry dry leaves
    whether the Pakeha marine authorities would sell
    us back ephemeral Maori land (now exposed to bird,
    bleached crab and shrimp) lying somewhere between
    low-water mark and high.

A pounding gavel is the sun today — a brassy auctioneer:
    the sea, his first assistant. Of this, no instant
    favour offered me in stint. I cushion my elbows
    deeper in sand. I'm the only bidder.
    For this beautiful piece of land/seascape, I will
    start the bidding at twenty falling axes per square
    centimetre, said the sun looking hard at me for an
    earlobe twitch, or, other sign.
    Get stuffed, I reply, holding my middle finger
    straight up — turning it. Slowly.

Idly I think, that after the eleven o'clock prayers
    tomorrow (and before lunch) my cousin will have
    gone to ground.
    'They may ban tangi-hanga in the future,' I say
    to him. 'Right now you're doing your job. This
    moment is forever as the splayed fingers of the hand
    drawn together, like a fist.' I look up at the sun
    and blink. The sun is beside itself, dancing. There
    are two of them.

The Magpies

When Tom and Elizabeth took the farm
The bracken made their bed,
And *Quardle oodle ardle wardle doodle*
The magpies said.

Tom's hand was strong to the plough
Elizabeth's lips were red,
And *Quardle oodle ardle wardle doodle*
The magpies said.

Year in year out they worked
While the pines grew overhead,
And *Quardle oodle ardle wardle doodle*
The magpies said.

But all the beautiful crops soon went
To the mortgage-man instead,
And *Quardle oodle ardle wardle doodle*
The magpies said.

Elizabeth is dead now (it's years ago);
Old Tom went light in the head;
And *Quardle oodle ardle wardle doodle*
The magpies said.

The farm's still there. Mortgage corporations
Couldn't give it away.
And *Quardle oodle ardle wardle doodle*
The magpies say.

DINAH HAWKEN

The Issue of Water

A life could be simple, it could be gushing like a spring,
it could be surging and cascading, swirling and rippling

like a river sweeping down to the sea: it is an issue
of fluency, the mother tongue, the first murmurings,

it is an issue of gentleness, giving, yet never giving
up the task of smoothing hardness, it is an issue

of purity, and of reflection, it is the issue of pure silver
coming as a colour into a dark world and moving

with such force and such beauty that we, standing beside it,
love what is coming and go willingly where it's going.

BRIAN TURNER

Alp

The alp at the end of the street
— *Stevens' Notebooks*

The alp at the end of the street
is known to all
as His Imperious Majesty

moody   radiant   properly aloof
and crowned   sometimes
by heavy-weight cloud

and although he likes to wear
a robe
of royal blue

pomp is not his true style
except when he's enthroned
beneath brilliant stars

on summer nights
reflecting the edgy light
of the moon

that rolls above him
a royally minted gold coin
and each generation of townsfolk knows

that whenever
grandeur's required
it's over to him

Aftermath

On a narrow shelf,
between steep hillside and sea,
small stones pack flat
forming a track where we walk
as the storm lessens,
and hear waves hushing
as though they scold the beach
above a deeper roar.
Cicadas rasp endless
questions at the trees
as the day grows hot
and the hills more overbearing
in their spinning heights.
You walk ahead,
past wild poppies and sedge,
your thoughts too widely cast,
your steps too brisk
for me to stay at your side
as separately we search
the flotsam above a boiling tide.
When we turn for home,
though comforted at meeting again,
our words are wind-driven
and stark as these cliffs
where no quarter is asked,
no real shelter given.

The Old Man's Example

These drifting leaves, for instance
That tap my shoulder
Come along with us, they say
There are one or two questions
We should like to ask you

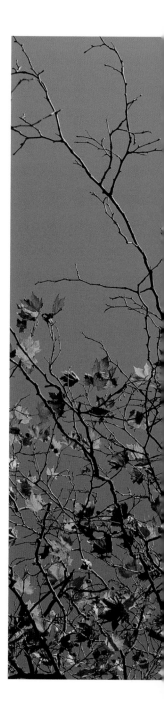

STEPHANIE DE MONTALK

Violinist at the Edge of an Ice Field

At first only silence,

and then slowly a dull roar
as if sediment is rising
from past climates
and ridges of soil
are shifting the bedrock,

and the scrape of horsehair
on resin, or a string which has yet
to be tightened
and could be grains of ice
squeezing the air,

a crevasse stretching,

or a solidified stream adjusting
to shear stress
and the immediate prospect
of decoupling,

and she knows she will need
to loosen herself up,

take herself down
to the level of science,

dismiss the mythical beast
beneath the surface
and try to believe
the glacier is little more
than hexagonal plates, needles
and stars which have lost
their sharp edge
and developed an interesting
crystalline structure,

that the atomic
arrangement of ice is boring
and best described as
a system of circles

and that, according to quantum theory,
this moment, this second,
this aged and uncertain
stretch of the planet

is only the tip of an iceberg
and computers
can handle anything.

In danger now of travelling too far
she places the laws of physics on hold,

tells herself
that in times of extremity
recollection of pleasure
can be useful

and thinks about her garden—
her sprinkler teasing the lawn,

the wide hips of her roses
swaying across fences,

her daphne growing wild
and covered with cobwebs—

and Stravinsky—the opera,
the concert, the silent
explosion...

no! she cancels Stravinsky
and returns to the cobwebs.

Here, she assumes the weighted
excellence of a spider,

imagines she has segmented
legs which will grow again
if she breaks them,

produces silk,

slides herself onto the ice,
her body tiny and slender,
her tongue lined with teeth,

applies her crampons and axe
to the surface
and starts picking her way
across the river—

sharp, connected and deadly.

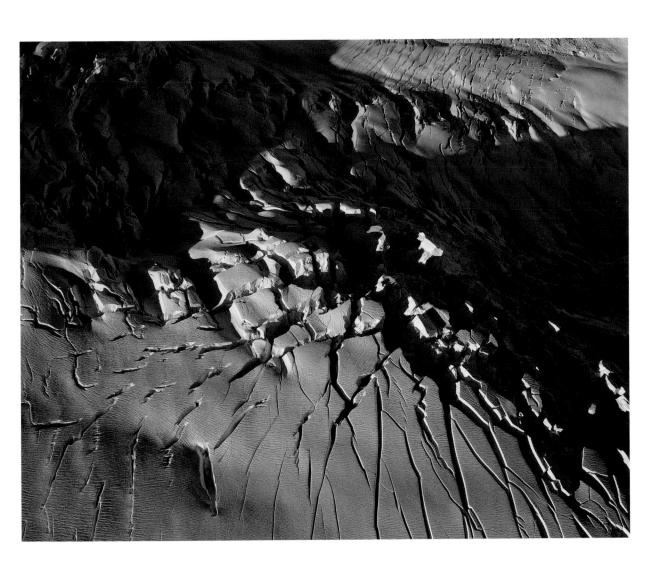

A White Gentian

Remember Ruapehu,
that mountain, six months ago?
You sat in an alpine hut
sketching scoria, red
rusted outcrops in the snow.

I climbed some southern peak
and made up the sort of song
men climbing mountains sing:
how, no longer your lover,
I knew it was over.

I thought I'd try out my song
when I returned that evening
as though there were nothing wrong.
Instead I brought a flower down
smelling of the mountain.

CILLA McQUEEN

Luncheon Cove

It was so calm in Dusky Sound
that Captain Cook requested
luncheon served ashore

beside the frothing pool
of a stream tumbling out of the bush
where sunlight filtered down

and cool air sprang
from amber peaty water, edged
with rock and fern.

His linen white, his table set with silver,
Captain Cook had an eerie, solitary feeling,
as if he had set foot on the moon.

Snow

A crime so frequent, so huge
of fraud and camouflage
would make it seem almost natural
the hurt world lying forever
                              locked in plaster
with some remembering the green
                              underneath,
others never forgetting the
                    fracture.

Flood

In the back country
hard rain
is bucketing

Here
in the narrowing light
the river bellows
fatly

From high ground
I mark
twin rows of willow
dishevelled arms
clutching drunk roots
hoarding
bits of old bridge-planking
the body of a beast
puff-bellied
hind feet sticking out

I ask:
when will the waters clear
the eels breathe easy again?

Shall I be able to ford
the river soon: visit
a lean Aunt?

Waiotapu

Pools laced with brilliant sulphides
arsenic, antimony and mercury.

Starlings leave their eggs
warming in the earth.

Alizarin crimson, cadmium, splashes of cool blue
colours crystalise on the cliff face.

Pigments bubble from the ground
steam streaks over the sky.

Pied stilts leave trails of tiny footprints
star-shaped indentations in the clay.

DINAH HAWKEN

Talking to a Tree Fern

1.
You're not ashamed of your past.
It hangs there in rust-coloured layers
and you curve out of it
fully at ease.

2.
Behind you the bay
sports expensive speed boats. More and more
they force their vibrations right up
your root-tips.

3.
You used to live here with other natives.
Now willows and poplars flickering gold
have proudly established themselves.

4.
I've heard you discussed as an item
of our international trade. They
conceive of you standing in each
pebble garden of suburban Los Angeles.

5.
The man at the back
has asked how much I care about you.
He says you impede his view.

6.
In the bush near here
you gather in tight bunches
your pasts hanging down and spreading
over the ground like soft mats.
I want to crawl under there.
I need to know what you're chatting about.

7.
Rowing out as usual
to the calmest part of the lake
I hear a chain-saw preening itself
and sense the spikes stiffening on your trunks.

8.
Once I saw you at a Marist Centre
stiff and brittle like an empty erection,
no fronds, no flow.
Mary was cramped into a grotto nearby
totally into pleasing God.

9.
I was just wondering whether
Christ had risen again this year or not
(Good Friday was April Fool's Day)
when I saw three fantails fooling around
in your fronds, in the rain.

10.
Under your dark arms
that night with no moon
I decided to let my life
climb up quietly
like the rata on your trunk.

11.
It leans so superbly
your long black trunk
perhaps it is frightening
the man at the back.

12.
Suddenly, in the city,
staked into a neat fence
you poke out your black tongue.
Keep coming and coming
back into my life.

CHARLES BRASCH

Forerunners

Not by us was the unrecorded stillness
Broken, and in their monumental dawn
The rocks, the leaves unveiled;
Those who were before us trod first the soil

And named the bays and mountains; while round them spread
The indefinable currents of the human,
That still about their chosen places
Trouble the poignant air.

But their touch was light; warm in their hearts holding
The land's image, they had no need to impress themselves
Like conquerors, scarring it with vain memorials.
They had no fear of being forgotten.

In the face of our different coming they retreated,
But without panic, not disturbing the imprint
Of their living upon the air, which continued
To speak of them to the rocks and the sombre, guarded lakes.

The earth holds them
As the mountains hold the shadows by day
In their powerful repose, only betrayed by a lingering
Twilight in the hooded ravines.

Behind our quickness, our shallow occupation of the easier
Landscape, their unprotesting memory
Mildly hovers, surrounding us with perspective,
Offering soil for our rootless behaviour.

Pinnacle Ridge, Mt Ruapehu
in memory of Colin Hill

The last rock at the top that for a time
caps the rocks below is where we stand,
also for a time. The summit of the ridge.

Pebble, boulder and stone slab arrange
a precedence. A backbone and a skull.
Sooner or later, wind-worn, flaked by ice,

or kicked to bits by a boot, the line alters.
The next rock along becomes the new summit.
We search for the safe way down. The fall

comes years later, in a bed or an armchair,
a seat in a café, a patch of shade on the lawn
where you lean your back against a tree.

The view across the peaks always ends
at the wall of the sky, a bedroom door,
a prospect across a street and no farther,

a garden hedge. Calcium, phosphorus —
a ridge of minerals rising to a bone summit
where the eyes squint for the least perilous

descent, an outlook across a valley rattling
with pebbles and boulders. Your death rearranges
the view. Sitting safely beyond that place,

that time, suddenly you are flung into the sky.
I remember you as the shape of an eyelash.
A curved shadow of stone dislodged on the climb.

A.R.D. FAIRBURN

The Estuary

The wind has died, no motion now
in the summer's sleepy breath. Silver the sea-grass,
the shells and the driftwood, fixed in the moon's vast crystal.
Think: long after, when the walls of the small house
have collapsed upon us, each alone,
far gone the earth's invasion
the slow earth bedding and filling the bone,
this water will still be crawling up the estuary,
fingering its way among the channels, licking the stones;
and the floating shells, minute argosies
under the giant moon, still shoreward glide
among the mangroves on the creeping tide.

The noise of gulls comes through the shining darkness
over the dunes and the sea. Now the clouded moon
is warm in her nest of light. The world's a shell
where distant waves are murmuring of a time
beyond this time. *Give me the ghost of your hand:*
unreal, unreal the dunes,
the sea, the mangroves, and the moon's white light,
unreal, beneath our naked feet, the sand.

September

The mountain leaps, and stands
breaking horizons. It is the first
land out of falling waters, the wind

finds it like a discovering dove.
In the wheeling light it is still,
construing containment, poise
from the inchoate idiom of the earth.

No flower was white before this
blossoming of snow, no September
sharp with spring until this morning.
I shall learn the lessons of God
from the mountain; it has entered
my imagination: eternal indifference,
eternal scope, eternal reprieve.

The Sea Question

The sea asks 'How is your life now?'
It does so obliquely, changing colour.
It is never the same on any two visits.

It is never the same in any particular
Only in generalities: tide and such matters
Wave height and suction, pebbles that rattle.

It doesn't presume to wear a white coat
But it questions you like a psychologist
As you walk beside it on its long couch.

JOHN NEWTON

Opening the Book

You open the book
& there unfolds a road   its skin is blue, it is summer
the heat   that dances in its hollows turns

into water.   You ride it in the vehicles of strangers:
homesteads & haybarns   dusty yellow sheeptrucks
convoy of soldiers in jungle greens returning

from an exercise
slipping past their polarised windscreens;
you draw from them splinters   of lives made of words

though you never take your eyes off the mountains.
The mountains reach out to embrace you
they fold their blue ankles

they give birth to rivers, they
can even crouch like tigers if that's the way you
want them: they are a story you tell

about yourself, a story you are journeying
into, which swallows you.   You leave
the road, then   you honour the logic of ridges

& gorges, of funnels, of slotted
stone chimneys   You startle a huge bird
nesting in the riverbed, climbing on slow

cream & ash coloured wings   & you follow
as it disappears
inland, you tunnel to the spine of the island

& bury yourself   alive, with your possessions, this
curved sky, this whisper of ice-cloud
this magic mountain slamming shut behind you.

IAIN LONIE

Proposal at Allans Beach

Basalt capes
thrust into the sea, the sea
curls back intimately
into the land, celebrating
a moody marriage. The wind here
saws into flesh like cord
but just around the sandhills
a small inland sea
dotted with maimais calmly sends
the sun back to heaven.
Even in winter you can lie
on its hard white beach
naked as if you'd just crawled
up from the sea like a fish with legs
and were looking around for a mate.
But up there above the ridges
it's always going on: the air
dividing, and pouring mist
down ngaio gullies, making sheep
get up and move, unveiling contours
taking them away again.
The whole place is a test site.
I've been bringing
people here for 20 years—
sometimes with a hard question
mostly to see how we match up
to its absolute background.
It never fails. Walk with someone
from the flax-hung cliff at one end
to the tidal creek at the other
and you'll know for sure
what's biting both of you
whether you could be friends for life
and lesser domestic truths. Of course
I had to be brought here once myself

on a particularly uninviting day.
Squinting up the dark green slopes
I knew I'd come home. Later
I sat by the lagoon a whole
sunfilled September day and planned
the work of a decade. And once
I came here with a friend and the rain
blew back into our faces and told us
we could never be the lovers
we thought we wanted to be.
I'm never alone here—
the place is full of ghosts.
With luck, you might see one
swimming naked in a rock pool
on the greyest day of the year.
It is a place for strong attachments:
friends, lovers, children.
I can't promise much
but you won't forget having been here
nor who you came with, and all
that followed, if it followed.

ALISTAIR TE ARIKI CAMPBELL

Kapiti

Kapiti An island near Cook Strait once the stronghold of
Te Rauparaha (1770-1849)

This island is alive with ghosts.
Tonight every leaf is an ear
attuned to your heartbeat,
every stick a spear
gripped by a crouching figure...
Their eyes glint
on the moonlit hillsides,
and their oiled bodies
bending towards you in their hundreds
gleam like flax...
Listen!
What is that sound
like the sound of waves on the rocks?
But there is no wind —
even the sea is asleep.
Listen!
The sea begins to wake in its wide bed
and whispers of war.
A thousand paddles shatter
the drowning moon,
a bridge of war canoes
spans the troubled sea
between Kapiti and the mainland...
It is no use.

Numbers cannot save you.
Nothing can save you now
but your swift paddles.
Te Rauparaha is a god
and Kapiti is his backbone.
Even the moon is his ally.

Men of the mainland,
be counselled and turn back.
Your streams are full of eels
and your valleys throb with pigeons
that are yours for the taking...
What tempted you to Kapiti?
Your wives are hot and willing
and will approve far more
than the scowling Ngati Toa
the adroitness of your stick play...
Aue! It is too late.
Already steam rises from your heads
as from an oven,
and the maddened Rangihaeata
roasts alive his suppliant kinsman
Rangimairehau...
Enough — it is done!
Mothers, put on the leaves of mourning —
wail for your sons.
Weep, widows,
slash your foreheads.
Howl, depleted tribes,
for your dishonoured manhood
whose bones lie scattered
on the shores of Kapiti.

Weathered Rocks

Poetry is a music made of images
    Worded one in the similitude of another,
Chaining the whole universe to the ecstasies
    Of humanity, its anguish and fervour.

But there shall be no equivalent
    Of these fire-wrought and water-worn boulders,
Tattoo'd and stained, silvered, denigrated,
    Rusted and empurpled by exposure
To ocean-salted south and east winds
Unremittingly sweeping over these headlands;

Since in the bosom of this volcano
    The fires abated, died down, and were exhausted,
Fretted by aurelian and grey moulds,
    Encrusted with frilled lichens, pale, glaucous;
Giving pittance to lissom tussock grasses
And twisted brambles, from invisible crevasses.

Rock, thorn, cryptogram, each has significance,
    Each makes contribution to eternal parabole;
And we are kin, compounded of the same elements,
    Alike proceeding to an unknown goal;
And they are secret to themselves as I am secret to myself,
    And I think they have no part in my dole;

And shall another estimate the influence
    Of mass, form, colour, on individual soul,
Or relate my smitten heart-throb,
    Beholding these things, to cosmic diastole?
But deep is the given peace, when informed particular
    Has respect unto the dignity of the whole.

High Country Weather

Alone we are born
    And die alone;
Yet see the red-gold cirrus
    Over snow-mountain shine.

Upon the upland road
    Ride easy, stranger:
Surrender to the sky
    Your heart of anger.

Magpie Crooning

Cold like the cold southern ocean,
and cold like the flatterer's stone,
she shivers and shifts and lifts her gaze
to the bird's mixed-up view of the morning.
Stewart Island, we call this place,
where we plan to go one day, bush
and a crescent of sand, a memory,
some sort of memory of a face,
and the woman listens for a moment or two
then calls the children in to dinner.
They sit at the table while she swims
in silence at the bottom of a wave.
'If you see this woman, you will go to heaven.
If you see her children, you will travel.
If you smile in English, they will sing.'
But no one does anything,
only the macrocarpa with its lonely shuffle,
making at least a hundred yards along the coast
— almost lost, but you bring a mind
to the mystery of things like this
and sing a song to make the branches miss you,
making a shadow flap towards your hand.
Sheet music! Light of a star,
light of the moon, shells of their brightness.
You walk on the shore and see the children,
single son, single daughter,
and you glimpse her at midnight
and you don't know what to say.
So cold and you don't know what to say.
(You join the orchestra and sail away,
blue postcard on the water.)

ACKNOWLEDGEMENTS

Craig Potton Publishing gratefully acknowledges permission to reproduce these poems from the following authors and publishers:

James K Baxter – from *Selected Poems* by James K. Baxter, ed Weir, Oxford University Press, Australia and New Zealand, 1985; reproduced by permission of J.C. Baxter

Ursula Bethell – from *Collected Poems*, Victoria University Press, Wellington, 1997

Jenny Bornholdt – from *Miss New Zealand*, 'West Coast' sequence, Victoria University Press, 1997

Charles Brasch – from *Collected Poems*, Oxford University Press, 1984; with permission from Alan Roddick and the Estate of Charles Brasch

Meg Campbell

Alistair Te Ariki Campbell – from *Kapiti: Selected Poems 1947-1971*, 'Sanctuary of Spirits', Pegasus Press, Christchurch, 1972

Glenn Colquhoun – from *The Art of Walking Upright*, Steele Roberts, Wellington, 1999

Allen Curnow – from *Early Days Yet*, 'Trees, Effigies, Moving Objects' sequence, Auckland University Press, Auckland, 1997

Ruth Dallas – from *Collected Poems*, University of Otago Press, Dunedin, 1987

John Dickson – from *What Happened On The Way To Oamaru*, Untold Books, Christchurch, 1986

Maurice Duggan – with permission from the Estate of Maurice Duggan

Lauris Edmond – from *Selected Poems 1975-2000*, Bridget Williams Books, Wellington, 2001; with permission from the Literary Estate of Lauris Edmond

A.R.D. Fairburn – with permission from the A.R.D. Fairburn Literary Estate

Janet Frame – 'Snow' from *The Pocket Mirror*, Pegasus Press, 1968; 'The End' first published in the *New Zealand Listener*, August 28, 2004; with permission from the Janet Frame Literary Trust

Rhian Gallagher – from *Salt Water Creek*, Enitharmon Press, London, 2003

Denis Glover – from *Selected Poems*, Victoria University Press, 1995; 'Lake, mountain, tree' from 'Sings Harry' sequence, 'The Scene' from 'Arawata Bill' sequence, with permission from Pia Glover and the Denis Glover Literary Estate

Dinah Hawken – from *Oh There You Are Tui!*, Victoria University Press, 2001

Sam Hunt – from *Collected Poems 1963-1980*, Penguin Books (NZ) Ltd, Auckland, 1980

Kevin Ireland – from *Anzac Day*, Hazard Press, Christchurch, 1997

Michael Jackson – from *Duty-Free: Selected Poems, 1965-1988*, McIndoe, Dunedin, 1989

Andrew Johnston – from *The Sounds*, Victoria University Press, 1996

Iain Lonie – from *Winter Walk at Morning*, Victoria University Press, 1991; with permission from Iain Lonie's literary executor

Bill Manhire – from *Collected Poems*, Victoria University Press, 2001

Fionnaigh McKenzie

Cilla McQueen – 'Low Tide, Aramoana' from *Homing In*, McIndoe, 1982; 'Luncheon Cove' from *Markings*, University of Otago Press, 2000

Stephanie de Montalk – from *The Scientific Evidence of Dr Wang*, Victoria University Press, 2002

John Newton

Gregory O'Brien – from *Winter I Was*, Victoria University Press, 1999

Naomi O'Connor

Vincent O'Sullivan – from *Butcher & Co*, Oxford University Press, 1977

Chris Orsman – from *Ornamental Gorse*, Victoria University Press, 1994

Kerry Popplewell

Elizabeth Smither – from *The Tudor Style*, Auckland University Press, 1993

Kendrick Smithyman – from *Stories about Wooden Keyboards*, Auckland University Press/Oxford University Press, 1985; with permission from M. Edgcumbe

Brian Turner – 'Alp', 'Crossing the Canterbury Plains' and 'Place' from *All That Blue Can Be*, McIndoe 1989; 'Far North' from *Beyond*, McIndoe 1992

Hone Tuwhare – from *Deep River Talk*, Godwit Press, Auckland, 1993; with permission from Random House NZ Ltd

Ian Wedde – from *The Commonplace Odes*, Auckland University Press, 2001

Craig Potton Publishing has made every effort to trace the copyright holders of all material contained in this book and attribute the correct acknowledgements. If any omissions have occurred, we would appreciate being contacted directly to rectify the mistake.

PHOTOGRAPH CAPTIONS

Pages 6–7   Ruth Dallas, *Deep in the Hills* – Preservation Inlet, Fiordland National Park

Pages 14–15   Denis Glover, *Lake, Mountain, Tree* – Nor'west Lake, Fiordland National Park

Pages 16–17   Glenn Colquhoun, *Collecting Pipi* – Awaroa, Abel Tasman National Park

Pages 18–19   Brian Turner, *Crossing the Canterbury Plains* – North Canterbury

Pages 20–21   Dinah Hawken, *Hope* – Whirinaki, Central North Island

Pages 22–23   James K. Baxter, *At the Franz Josef Glacier* – Franz Josef Glacier, Westland/ Tai Poutini National Park

Pages 24–25   Janet Frame, *The End* – Nugget Point, Catlins Coast

Pages 26–27   Vincent O'Sullivan, *Still Shines When You Think Of It* – Australasian Harrier, (Chris Rudge/Hedgehog House)

Pages 28–29   Hone Tuwhare, *Haiku (1)* – Stream, Whirinaki, Central North Island

Pages 30–31   Maurice Duggan, *In the Territory* – Paparoa Range, Paparoa National Park

Pages 32–33   Lauris Edmond, *Lake Idyll* – Lake Taupo

Pages 34–35   Chris Orsman, *Ornamental Gorse* – Gorse, Westport

Pages 36–37   Brian Turner, *Key Summit* – Key Summit, Fiordland National Park (Rob Brown)

Pages 38–39   Jenny Bornholdt, *Make Sure* – Forest, Te Urewera National Park

Pages 40–41   Iain Lonie, *A Summer at Purakanui* – Kelp, Stewart Island (Rob Brown)

Pages 42–43   Kendrick Smithyman, *Waitomo* – Waitomo Caves

Pages 44–45   Allen Curnow, *A Dead Lamb* – West Coast, Auckland

Pages 46–47   Rhian Gallagher, *Waitohi* – Cabbage trees, Golden Bay

Pages 48–49   Ursula Bethell, *Candour* – Upper Tasman Glacier, Aoraki/Mount Cook National Park